I AM ENOUGH

An Empowerment Journey

Through Poetry & Affirmations

Expanding Your Zest for Life!

Written by

Wanda D. Hollis

I Am Enough, An Empowerment Journey Through Poetry & Affirmations Expanding Your Zest for Life!

Copyright © 2015 by Wanda D Hollis

Printed in the United States of America

ISBN 978-0-692-71290-0

Cover design by Crystal Easley

Dedication

I dedicate this book to my children
Brian and Aaliyah
Let no one tell you what you can't do!
Always remember God's promise,
All things are possible if you believe!

Acknowledgements

To God be the glory, if not for my Father in heaven I would not be here. I know and believe that writing and inspiring others is a gift from God. I am extremely humbled and forever grateful.

An extraordinary thanks to my Momma for the words she whispered to me as a child, "I am smart, I am beautiful and I can do anything", those seeds she planted is why this book exist. She has always believed and supported me through every adventure of my life.

A very special thanks to My Grandparents, My Brothers, My Sister, for always being there, your love is priceless.

To Lawanda, Ricky, Salimah, Rena, Johnny, Carina, and Ruben for always answering the phone and listening to a new poem.

Thanks to all of my friends, and family who encouraged and inspired me to push through all of the obstacles and setbacks.

To my beloved and late Pastors Martha Jean the Queen Steinberg of the Home of Love and Jack Boland of the Church Of Today. Their teaching and mentoring played a major role to my spiritual growth as a woman. The teaching and memories of them are forever engraved in my heart and spirit.

Foreword

In Wanda D. Hollis's first book of poems, *I AM Enough*, Hollis breaks into our consciousness, like any good drama, with a bang. The first line of *Confession*, her first poem, fits nicely into the confessional poetry niche: *"I Ain't Gonna Lie (I Get High)"*. In great contrast to introductory poem, *A Hole In My Stiletto* is the second poem of this volume. The *Stiletto* poem is a laundry list of sorts that depicts the daily routines of a business woman. While *Confession* examines a life gone terribly wrong. *Stiletto* examines the climb out of chaos with one foot still in the proverbial gutter. If you want to neatly categorize these poetic offerings you will be hard pressed to do so. By mimicking a roller coaster ride, Hollis effectively expresses emotion, empathy, depth and the surface of life.

A broad selection of poems in *I Am Enough,* displays traditional subject matter often found in black poetry, such as family, special moments, dramatic monologues, portraits and problematic images. Hollis wraps them all in a blanket of music and rhythm. Her's are narrative songs, powerful yet not jarring. They are explicit reminders of the noble human struggle. Not quite the same as Robert Hayden's made-up words, like *"fear starts a-murbling"* in his poem *Runagate, Runagate*. Hollis still manages to intrigue with witty section title assemblages such as "Taking My Car Out of Park" and "Who Moved My Dream?"

In the very last poem *I Am Enough*, Hollis offers a final push of encouragement to the invisible reader. *I AM Enough* is organized into five distinct sections with a closing appendix of 107 affirmations in which the title poem *I Am Enough* comes in at number 87 on the list. By this placement Hollis affirms that once you realize that you are enough, there is yet more to come.

Wanda Hollis has written a book, accompanied by a CD voice recording, which runs true to the roots of black history's poets. It has been written that Langston Hughes pioneered the integration of blues and jazz rhythms with lyrics in his poems, since the 1920s, music has been as indispensable to the art of poetry writing as sunlight to a plant that produces flowers. In this vein *I Am Enough,* Hollis integrates both the lyrical and the musical aspects into her spoken words. In conclusion, I suggest you put on your best dancing shoes, relax and enjoy the *I AM Enough* ride.

Alice Shapiro, Poet Laureate of Douglasville, Georgia

Table of Contents

Section 1   **A Compromising Position**   **9**

Confession   10

A Hole in My Stiletto   15

Homeless   17

Adore   22

Entangled   24

60 Seconds to Self-Destruct   27

Who's My Daddy?   29

Passing Scars   30

Sing To Me   32

Recoup   34

Section 2   **Taking My Car Out Of Park**   **36**

Keep It Moving   37

Almost There   39

Trail Blazer   40

Crossroads   41

Proceed   43

No Instructions Necessary   45

Wrong Way   46

Playhouse   47

Hell   50

Money Time   51

Section 3   **Making A Fashion Statement**   **56**

The Lady   57

Forecast   60

InStyle   61

Stained   63

Gloveless   70

Unconditional   73

Who's Watching?   74

Perfect Fit   76

Rainbow   78

Dare To Be More   79

Section 4   **Risky Business**   **82**

27 Ways 2 Love   83

In Time   84

What Really Matters   85

Promise   87

What If?   88

Live & Learn   89

Pure   92

Testing Testing   93

You Smell That   94

.Com   97

Section 5   **Who Moved My Dream?**   **101**

Awakening   102

Day Dream   104

Me   105

Higher Learning   106

All Aboard   107

Fallen   108

Mistaken Identity   109

Committed   111

Living   112

I am Enough   113

107 Affirmations   **119**

About the Author   **129**

A COMPROMISING POSITION

Life will find you in places where you may be unsure of.
Remember your emotional capabilities always wants to expand.
I believe our capacity to grow comes from our challenges and
there are times when the light doesn't glow brightly
but just remember change
is just around the corner.

CONFESSION

I ain't gonna lie -I get high
There's nothing I wouldn't do for it

There is nothing I wouldn't do for it!

I would marry, divorce and become a virgin all over a again
I would kick down doors for it
Beat, heat, and seduce the streets for it
Build sanctuaries, monument and cemeteries for it

Search the highways, the by way, freeway and expressways

I would travel by boat, plane or train
I would move to New York, London, and Spain
I would circle the world, the stars, the moon and galaxy for it
I ain't gonna lie -I get high

There's nothing I wouldn't do for it
Steal for it
Kill for it
Borrow for it
And beg for it
Lay down my life for it
Pray and meditate for it
Commit a sin for it

I would stay in the ghetto, the suburbs or country for it

I would campaign and clown for it

I would be lock up, caught up, and cooped up

Stirred up, sipped up and shook up for it

I ain't gonna lie -I get high

There's nothing I wouldn't do for it

I would jump in the lake for it

Fish in the river for it

And skim the sea for it

I would scale the empire state building for it

Stay in the jungle or sleep in a cave for it

Impersonate a prisoner

Or pretend to be a nun for it

I ain't gonna lie- I get high

There's nothing I wouldn't do for it

I would walk, hike, ride and run for it

Fly, roll, crawl, and cry for it

Walk tight ropes, Climb Mountains,

Go down in valleys and allies and train cats for it

Do You Know How Hard It Is to Train a Cat?

Beat bushes and cut down trees for it

Start wars or make peace for it

Dig a ditch or get lynch for it

Build up or tear down for it
Succeed or fail for it
I ain't gonna lie -I get high

There's nothing I wouldn't do for it
I would call on a doctor, a lawyer, and a priest for it
Jump on a bike, fly a kite, and surf for it
Hitchhike or sky dive

(And keep in mind…I'm not too fond of heights)

But, I would celebrate and dedicate my life for it!

I ain't gonna lie-I get High
There's nothing I wouldn't do for it!

Please remove the needle from my vein
And give me oxygen of sound to my brain
Supply me with the flow of adjective and adverbs

Conjunctions, nouns and pronouns
Preposition, verbs and contractions
Contracting, contracting, contracting

Giving birth to the resurrection of my soul
I salute to you to

My past

My Present

And my future

Sprinkle water on my forehead

Giving me a Baptism, Christening and a *Bar Mitzvah*

For my life

There's nothing I wouldn't do for it!

I ain't gonna lie! -I get High

There is nothing I wouldn't do -to have this pen- in my hand

Just to write for you

A poem, short story, screenplay or documentary

I ain't gonna lie -I get HIGH

Because to me this is the greatest high!

And I salute to you

A meeting to remember

Alphabets get twisted and phases are distorted

An entanglement of misquotes and empty pages

Still I search for my pen to guide me

Through cyclones and hailstorms

With thoughts of rolling into solutions that soothe

Predictions that meditate on satisfying outcomes

Or should I say come-outs

Stepping out of closets and freeing myself
With the power of this pen on the run
Across the pages again and again
Not afraid to tell the story

The pen has become -my best friend
Its reward is the collaboration of the pen
Meet my tablet
So let the stories begin!

Yea I get high!

A HOLE IN MY STILETTO

5a.m. I awake

Meditate, a brisk walk

OG coffee in my cup

Shower time-bubbles lather

Oil me up, matching bra and panties

Red suit will do with matching shoes.

Emails received and sent, phone calls follow-ups too

Bag is packed, with papers needed

To the office, post office and pick up flyers

And to the cleaners
Clients to meet, smile in place

Don't forget to compliment.

I journey all day, on my feet

Jump in taxicabs over and over again

Big smile on my face- ok to pretend

Is that a hole in my stiletto?

Oh well, day's not over

Got a meet and greet at 8 pm

No time for stopping

Still so much work left to do

Must push pass this annoying hole, in my shoe!

Homeless

The words don't come easy, they don't come quick
I knew months ago it was coming to this
Homeless
Yes I said it

Homeless

It didn't bother me much when I walked away from my home of many years
All the up keep, too many rooms to tend to
Down size is what its call
That didn't really bother me at all

I chalked it up to a weight lifted, time to move on

I move to a new spot and that's when things got hot
So I pack up once again, but this time it was so different

My Stuff ...in storage or left behind

And, I had a plan but that fell through to
Now in a panic
Pressure
Don't know what to do

Homeless

Yes I said it

Homeless it such a simple word but hard to say,

I'll take all responsibility and know that it was the choice I made

But even with truth on track, it still got derailed

And smells so bad I just shake my head

Self-eluded pride- I don't want the world to know

Homeless

Homeless Webster describe it as having no home or permanent place of residence

So this is the place where life finds me at age 45

This is the place where I stare with my eyes filled with tears

And it hurts to breathe

I never thought it would happen to me

No one could have prepared me for all the emotion that invaded me

Unspeakable thoughts of suicide left me balled up in knots,

And paralyzing pictures hunted my dreams

leaving me in doubt

Homeless

It did something to my soul

It sunk my sense of stability it immobilized my movement

Bring everything to a halt

I was not just homeless
I had become less of everything, so I thought
Homeless was begin to defiled me
I was occupying space that wasn't mine
The bags I carried made me weary, weak and exhausted
All resources depleted, left vacated and closed for business
Just vacant

Homeless

Wow, what happen to my life? Is this the ultimate sacrifice?
Now I'm looking for a safe place to lay my head

And with family all around me emotion -don't get off me
I sank like -quicksand

Down, down, down into the devastation of displacement
With distinctive lines
No, no, no this is not a dream.
As I hasten to believe

Homeless

It was a night after an event; need to make it back to my shelter
And the only one that answered, my daughter-in-law

She can with little delay, but then asked if my two grandbabies could stay
She really needed to get to work and earn her pay- for the next day

I knew in my heart that it probable was bad to say yes,
but I said it any way

Immediately, the next day my mom blow a gasket
As soon as she realized my two little ones was on the couch
Her tone was sharp and it cut down to my core

And even as I offered an explanation- to explain the situation
She just snared and said she didn't care
Insisting, I need permission to bring my grandkids there
I was so disappointed for the way she scolded me

I expected her to be kind but it was just the opposite

Tear ran down my face as I started to hyperventilate
My temperature elevates, and thought I would flip

If I had a car I would leave
But I can't
If it weren't raining, I would walk
But, my babies would get wet
Just look at me can't jump in my ride because it not parked out side
Had to pawn it to pay the rent, and the money was never use for that intent
Got pinched
And that's what started on the cycle like a rat chasing cheese

Now with my vehicle tucked away folks call me everyday

They want their money or my ride back so I dodge the phone calls and hide

But in my heart I want to be free from phones and threatening message

I plead and beg tying to explain that I'm down- on my last leg

And I'm quickly getting to the point where I don't give a fuck

But allow me to continue with the story

No home, no car, no money

I forgot, my badd, I forgot

I was homeless but was reminded in that instant as my tears glistened

Just to be able to watch these two kids made my life seem normal

And after all it was family, so I thought

In my heart, I forget I was homeless but quickly was reminded of that

Where I didn't set the rules, homeless

No place to stay not for me, or my grandbabies

Even my tears let me down

As they rolled and rolled and rolled

Away from me like everything else had done

Homeless

ADORE

A mother's water breaks down
Outcome is baby yes beauty all around
We listen, the greatest sound

She craps on chewed pages
Trying to live on minimum wages, but
Landlord knocks, cops say vacate

Her pleads go unnoticed, please
Another day, another chance, dollars should flow
No, no she's got to go!

Gaps between meals, all notice
No offers yet to rest her head, tired
Of sink baths, slumber chairs

But still in search of

Dry places and laughter of good times

Rainbow has to appear, immediately

Not willing to become useless
But losing ground, her cries are silenced
As she trembles no sounds left

Enemy lines caught her unaware
And blinded by evidence despair to this

Now ain't that some shit
Homeless howls and blank stares
As lights dim and darkness sets in

She waves her flag surrendering to fear
Unemployment and soup lines overflow
She has to hold on to hope

For that baby born, Adore

The name-meaning gift, beloved
Where is kindness and generosity for Adore?
In alleyways and extended stays
Daylights and night waves on
Seasons change and mom still hangs on
And she still hangs on

Hanging on to the overflow
Blessed from the heavens above baby Adore
Her reason to hang on

Adore, Adore, Adore

ENTANGLED

I am not as naive as little red riding hood
Though I am not as brave as Michele Obama or
Coretta Scott King

Risking my life, to fight a cause
I think not but who knows?

Today I stand for the voiceless
The hopeless
The prisoners of unjust and lost souls

The penniless
The uninsured
The elderly we cast away
The enslaved categorized as mindless

I keep standing so they don't pass away
Time tells of paths to follow, will tomorrow ever come?

My heart beats to heat waves of yesterdays
Hopscotch
Lollipops
Penny candy
And skate parties

Looking for red lights in dungeons and kisses of sweet beats

Behind the candles meltdown

Wax everywhere

Roll bounce- roll bounce

Parking lots that misdirect, I can't squeeze-

My mind between the lines and box up my thoughts

I dream of the Pops I never knew

Did he look like me?

How did he walk?

How did he talk?

And why did he leave?

He's little girl fatherless

To crush thoughts on pavement and blackened concrete

Skid markers on upside down dreams

Mary Poppins, I don't know that chick

And my Fair Lady, doesn't give me justice

Just doesn't seem real to me

Can't get over the rainbow

Too cold in the desert

Sunbeams telling lies behind scenes

Wallpaper hiding art

Despaired to tricky things

Madness on the eclipse of harvesting moonlight

Plowed and pulled in all directions

Between rhythm and rhymes interludes

Of unsung prologue on steroids

Looking for my hero

Just looking for MY Hero

Have you seen MY HERO?

Don't judge me

So I kiss the street

Make vows to unknowns

In trenches is where I eat

Birth to babies discarded feces

Wrapped in brown paper bags

Watching buildings burn

As we all turn into ash!

60 SECOND TO SELF-DESTRUCT

Mission impossible on a hunt to find a clue

Check the pantry, by the TV and bathroom counter

The only places I've been

Recall back, maybe it was yesterday

60 second to self-destruct

Marry-go round, jerked to a sudden stop

Bumper to bumper sparks fly-

I'm caught

60 second to self-destruct

Car on fire, seat belt holds on

Blaze getting hotter, feels like 300 degrees

Stains of perspiration be-friends me

60 seconds to self-destruct

Following, dashboard and addiction

Hunting cigarettes wasn't worth the trip

Now look at me, should have read the label

60 seconds to self-destruct

WHO'S MY DADDY?

The complexity of DNA, a scientific fact
Sperm swims up stream, and Newton's law
What goes up must come down

Baby in the basket
Call up Maury, DNA doctors on speed dial
Free test to tell your story-

Deal too good to pass up

Now staged up, pictures all around

As the audience over looks

Here come test results, now
All heads are shook

She falls down to her knees

Rolling pins all on the floor

Shocked, swore you were the daddy

Now back to the drawing board.

PASSING SCARS

The mirror reflects scars of my pass lover

Tear drops-

Left tracks of hip-hop, lost in chaos

While I was serenaded on Cali's waves over San Francisco

And Montego Bay

With each tune he played I was caught off guard

He snatched my essences and made off with my heart

My heart torn out, he took and ran
My heart torn out, he took and ran
I guess that was always his plan

Because he just took it and ran
You laid down promises and walked out the door
My dreams fade into the melodies

And you watch a good girl misbehave

I can't pretend the pain doesn't sting

But to on lookers, all they see is bling

My heart torn out, he took and ran
My heart torn out, he took and ran
I guess that was always his plan

Because he just took it and ran
I was pass down and set aside
I wade in a pool of a little girls

Foolish pride
As I call on paramedics and plumbers

911 to stop the disillusion that continues to drain
911 to stop the disappointment running through my veins
My heart torn out, he took and ran
My heart torn out, he took and ran
I guess that was always his plan

Because he just took it and ran

He took it and ran
Yea, he took it and ran
My heart he took it and ran

SING TO ME

No music playing
Did I love you too much?
Were my caresses too tight?
Were my kisses too sweet?

These are the questions; I asked myself last night

As thoughts of when we were lovers
And I wanted no other, only you
To sing to me as my soul soared in flight
I frequently think back in time

When you said you were all mine
You painted flamboyant pictures of how our lives intertwined
We took walks in the park
Our hands interlock

We went on long rides
Picked flowers off countryside's
We ate off the same plate
Never could imagine how now

We don't even speak

So as I sit in the dark
I make love to my heart

Putting back broken pieces

As I keep on believing
That the best of me waits, for my new knight to save me
From the past pain inside, in need of a sweet lullaby

RECOUP

Compounded interest over-time

Now relax and unwind

Into my deposits of

Compounding interest over time.

Dividends due

Stocks rise and fall

Just got a call from my banker

I am overdrawn?

How did that happen?

Thought I kept a close watch

There has been a leak?

So I sprint in to stop

The deplete

And begin again

Compounding interest over time.

A Compromising Position

Write about it

1) What do you consider to be your worst situation in life and why?

2) What lessons did you learn from that situation?

3) How did you move pass that situation?

*KEEP GOING AND DON'T GIVE UP!

TAKING MY CAR OUT OF PARK

Move now!

The tow truck is coming through and if we are not careful,

to the impound is where we will end up

and no telling how costly it will be to get out!

KEEP IT MOVING

Relying on a relationship to comfort the confusion
Looking, seeking out memories of roasting marshmallows
And pillows fights
Inspired by my determination to succeed in my aspirations
Don't let go
I say to myself

Just one more chance
Just one more dance
To prove to myself
To prove to the world
That I can place passion with purpose
Mix miracles with mindset
Yes I can

So I'll keep it moving
So what
They told you no
Did it break you down? Did you plummet to the ground?

So what
They said not today
Did you stop breathing and forget how to endure?

So what
They said your ideal sounds extreme

Did it cause you to crumble and disable you to exist?

So what
They put you to the back of the bus
Did it stop from riding or cause you to fight?

I can make it this time as long as I keep the fire
I can stay in the game as long as I'm not willing to quit
I can overcome my fears and face the pain,
As long as I believe it's my time to win

I'll keep it movin until the job is done.

ALMOST THERE

As I hold on to sirens of serenity

I am obligated to release my divinity

As I walk, walk, walk, into my destiny

TRAIL BLAZER

Drenched in possibilities, parachuting into my purpose
Determined to march and run to the thump of my own drum
Devoted to serve with the fullness of love that breeds
Generously

As my trail blazes and dust delivers clues
Time keeps ticking and spinning around life's clock
Tic- tock minutes multiple and dirt turns into mud

Each breath in time will unfold my story
No one can play my part
I am the producer, director, and leading lady

The ending, I will design
Making sure to leave unforgettable memories
As I blaze the trail to my own story!

CROSSROADS

Did you get the news?
Doctors say you're terminally ill, that
You've only got just a few months to live

With your heart racing fast
You step on the gas, clutching the wheel
Out of control feeling, it's overwhelming
Too much to deal with as you panic and gasp

Air blowing through the windows
And in your mind to,
As you try to decide just what to do

Tears flowing, blouse dripping wet
Hands perspiring of sweat
And your heart feels like cardiac arrest

Then comes the calm in your spirit
You find endearing, a big sigh and a twinkle in your eye

As you breathe in deep you believe you can beat this
And in that moment your transformation begins
Growing stronger in the reflection of the great I am

Your tears become of happiness and a joyous validation
Your sadness sparks and immediate appreciation

Your confusion ignites a loyal dedication
Your worry has become a victory celebration

That anxiety no longer cripples you
Rather aids in the prosthesis to assist and equip you
This report turns into the biggest movement of your life

As the clock reads

No better time than the present your face displays delight
Now fight for your life, moving with the test
Let this diagnosis position you to live life limitless

Move on what you suspect is full happiness
Allow Gods goodness to empower you everyday

Be reminded of mercy
It has always cleaned up the messes and mistakes you've made
And while grace has always laid the path to see you through
Choosing a miracle certainly can happen to you

All you need to do is start living now with a purpose in your soul
Believing that God is knowing of all things
He is working on our behave and he never grows weary
For he has already secured your crown

As long as YOU stay believing!

PROCEED

I am undergoing a scientific experiment
Please stand by as I am disassembled and reconstructed
On beds that bleed and steam that rises high
Don't look away with judgment eye

A disgusted look from you have no ideal of all the shit I took

Does my behavior have you pickled?
Is that why you hold on to sign, march and protest?
Of decisions made of me,

Is this what you call democracy?

Where were the tears when the dam broke?
Drowning in water, too much to drink
City demolished, bodies forgotten on rooftops

Just where were your picked signs then?

Did that fail to turn your stomach?
From the outside in?
On scandals of too much to handle

Yea that right I am under construction
The sign is written on the mantle

And its ok, you don't approve
I don't agree with implants
And fake boobs

Risky business could be dangerous
But vanity is the fame you're after
So I'll just observe

As I relax in the decision I make

My body, my choose, my cross to bear
Fortunately for me
I hemorrhage forgiveness

And that includes me!

NO INSTRUCTIONS NECESSARY

Self-discovery is the best!

Let on one tell you differently

Your uniqueness

That's your Picasso to the world

Please allow us to observe it

Always just be you

WRONG WAY

On the heels of defeat

Your soles are worn down

Feet begin to bleed

But it is not over

Just stop and change direction

There's still plenty road *ahead*

PLAYHOUSE

She comes home shocked!

Hey, just how did you get into my playhouse?
Thought I took away your key and changed the locks
Now look at you rummaging through my thoughts

Are you serious, redecorating my space?

Removing my success pictures and *it's my time* clock from the wall
Where did you put my journal?
I know I left it here
And what about the novel I'm working on?

It was right beside the fridge, next to that
I Am Enough poem

Just how did you get into my playhouse?

Last I saw you, you were at the house of doubt
Had them all convinced
That watching TV made a whole lot of sense
Even had a schedule and a timer set
And a bet with your three cousins
Procrastinator, fear, and disbeliever
That we all would concede!
Give up and abandon our dreams

I swung from branch to branch quick

Getting out of there!

How did you get into my playhouse?

How did you make it pass Isaiah 54:17?

No weapon that is formed against thee shall prosper; and every tongue *that* shall

Rise against thee in judgment thou shalt condemn. This *is* the heritage of the

Servants of the LORD, and their righteousness *are* of me, saith the LORD.

And LORD, I do accept!

Amen!

What happen? Was my guard down?

Did I sleep too sound?

Or did you float into the window

When I was listening to my inspirational sounds

And reading my kindle?

I thought my vision board, my daily declarations,

And my positive self- talk had you blocked.

Again I ask, how did you get into my playhouse?

I counted on my liked mined friends, accountability coaches

And my righteous spiritual leaders- to keep you away

And lastly, I did depend on mentors and role models
And, of course my dream making buddies- to fill my play
But somehow you still managed, bounced into my house
Took a seat, as if you were invited
Oh no!

I don't think so; it's time for you to go.
Make sure you take all of your friends
Poverty, sickness, bitterness and confusion
Don't forgive lazy, conformity, and the oldest self-doubter
And did I mention procrastinator, people pleaser and non-believer

Get up…out of here!
Right now, it's time to go!
And this time, I'm using security, Matthew 19:26_
Jesus looked at them and said,
"With man this is impossible, but with God all things are possible."

So don't you even think about returning
To my Playhouse!

Hell

I am back from hell

And wow what a ride

Didn't think I would make it out

It was full with uncertainty and sham

And countless games of delusion

I am back from hell my mind ran an muck

Played trick on me got the joker's bad luck

They tried to kill me burn me up, feed my mind with false images -Offering suspicion, and self-pity, while insisting that it was good for me. I am back from hell, lost some friends on the way. I ate off the forbidden tree, now the biggest tummy ache-Poison ran through my brain but fortunate for me my saints were on the throne! Praying that I receive my share of mercy and grace...

I am back from hell; step in bad smells on the way

Some odors will always remain

To avert me of the jesters bag of tricks

The psychedelic color will raise curiosity,

But I won't fall for it

Unless I carelessly, take another ride

Back to hell, inside the corners of my mine

Money Time

Put God first
Thank him for his grace and mercy
And pray every day!
Take all talents to a new level

Cultivate- like cream churns, creating butter
Sweet cream spreading on toast, need of a little jelly
Let's go- get to this money

Tired of pockets picking up pennies
When too much money pushes- the city

All we must do is get to work- believing
Dreams are the wind that pulls the tugboat
And the choo choo trains, yes I Can!

Go get this money
It was then and still is
Written in the book of Lamb

First comes the word spoken-
The tongues- can extent
And create thing
The earth is proof
Just look around- it's in everything you do
So let's get this money

If you believe in the Father, like I do
And if his word rings true, to you
He said all things
That doesn't exclude
Getting to this money

As some bible totters will have you- believe
Pardon me but I'll just have to disagree
See my counsel promised me
The Father, The Son and the Holy Ghost

And every one of my heavenly Angles
I believe
When you see me, you see them

In all their glory
And as long as I walk this earth
I just want to deposit beautiful stories

This one features
"Getting to this money"
As I mentioned before-cultivate
Take your talents- and mix with believing
Always represent your best

Don't worry about the hater-
Again we all have a special job to do

Just keep getting to your money

Put your calendar on steroids
Design a master plan
Don't sleep on your dream

It was implanted long before

You made it to dry land
Picture your success before it's seen
Get dress to walk the red carpet
Expect the cameras flashing
It won't be a dream

On lookers will stare
Be sure to wave back

Knowing in your heart
That you are here because of
Faith, strength and tenacity
Even when others doubted you

So the money just- represents
Your passion behind the test
The victory- after defeat
The rise- after the fall

It is nothing more than the energy moving

Bringing big things your way
Open your hands, heart, and mind

Say I'm ready
To receive what's mine
And take your money
Use it with intelligently

So it can always yield a full return
Never lose focus of all the lessons you learn
Be a blessing to those
As they admire, what makes you strong
Thank you Father
For giving me my money

And enabling me to move on!

Taking My Car Out Of Park

Write about it

1) Who or what is slowing you down?

2) If you were to remove that situation from your life describe how life would be?

3) Are you taking responsibility for yourself and if not why?

*KEEP GOING AND DON'T GIVE UP!

MAKING A FASHION STATEMENT

Your ability to connect with yourself is priceless.
Remember you cannot separate yourself from
Integrity, Truth, Decisions and Love.
It's ok to be different!

THE LADY

So, the shape of her behind and the sway from side to side mesmerizes you

Don't be

You think you are impressed by the size of her breast and the feeling of the caress

Don't be

You admire the muscles in her thighs and the twinkle in her eyes

Don't be

You really quiver when you look at her lips- now stop that

Do you know why you are so turned on by what you see?

That outer look is what has you hooked

But surely you must know, she will up and go

She will leave you, just as quick as you taste that

She will break your heart and never look back

Unless, you detect the lady trapped inside

The lady

She will amaze and inspire you to reach heights that no climax can provide you

The lady

She will take your mind to places you never knew existed, opening secret doors to release your full ore

The lady

She will dance with you and plan with you in hopes that you discover all the man in you

The lady

She will build you up and fill your cup with treasures that are sure to bring out the best in you

The lady

She will push you and pull you, encouraging you to become all that God has planned for you

Look for the lady

Don't settle for her style it is only a camouflage,

Dig deep, is where you will find, the unleashing of her mind

Dig deep

Don't take a peek and run, wait for it

Dig deep

Look for the lady!

To paint a perfect picture

With dancing canvassing playing connect the dots

She glances up for guidance before picking a spot

Now realizing that it's her time

As she holds the paint brush in her hand

Sadly she spins down into spiraling rides

Paralyzing pictures, their colors are shaded gray

With hopes of color strokes- finding vivid tones

Praying that the pain fades away

She designs another picture featuring
Carousels in Brazil, Kaleidoscopes in Peru
Splashes in Spain and nights over Egypt

They'll be calling out her name
She smiles as the colors cooperate
The blending convinces her, let's celebrate
To paint the perfect picture

Just look
The great I am
Inside of the lady!

FORECAST

Thunderous forecasts to unknown pathways, mysteries of life
As sand keeps turning in the hourglass
Measurement of quality cannot be defined
Only grains of time and misplaced memories are held captive
In the crevices of ones mind

In the hunt to regain the pebbles far left behind
Still the journey continues, redefining each gain in time
As we take pride in delivering hot temperatures and clear skies
It is in those moments when life is worth living
Because so much is understood but unlike the earth it
sometimes quakes

We knew it was coming but waited to late
So now lack of preparation is the cause of this distasted
I urge you to follow your spirit and be led by your heart
God has a plan just for you, without any doubt

The design is perfected and the idea is intent
The rules cannot be broken although they can be bent
Watch out for bad weather but don't allow it to hold you back
Dress for a bright day just be sure to bring a change of clothes
Weather the forecast, because you can't predict the rain.

IN STYLE

What do you do with a collection of,

Albums, eight tracks and cassette tapes?

Like played out bell-bottoms and maxi skirts

Allowed to stay in your closet

Hoping to get another chance.

A chance to prove,

Style and sophistication

Never dies it just magnifies

On runways as men sit

Dazed and amazed to watch
So remember as you try
Throwing me away

New eyes rest on my old rags,

Delighted that I flaunted their way

They will assume I just stepped off

The pages of Essence, Ebony and Cosmo

Latest edition, chic so enchanting and refined

Heads will turn just to ask me

"Where have you been all my life?"
My reply, "Just hanging in the wrong closet
Yearning to make an entrance,
So do you like my style?"

STAINED

What's your favorite color?

It's it blue for Democrats

Or red for Republicans

Or is it the other way around

You see

I am colorblind

And I only keep up with sound

Vote for me is the tune that they all supply

Throwing us breadcrumbs, hoping to curve the hunger

Lessen the starvation the sadness it breeds throughout our homes
Throughout our streets

Treating us like monkey, walking the chimpanzee

As we rattle cages the pretend they don't see

What's your favorite color?

Are you sold out the newest voice?

Sounding pretty good, after all it wears a skirt

Should I be impressed?

Or do I rely on truth, hypocrisy

Government corrupted, big cities failing us

Afraid to leave their homes, doors kicked in

Fired the cops, and teachers too

School doors closing, my tears rolling, down

The town I grow up in- Detroit

Was once thriving and everyone knew

Now afraid to stop at red lights

Fearing both day and night

And some escape but not all can

Left behind to take a stand

Detroit made the top 10 again

As the most dangerous place to live!

Once was a town creating stars and motorcars

Not its six holding caskets and walking psychosis

I really can't believe this is happening to my city

And what would Coleman say?

I know he's rolling in his grave

Just what color do you choose?

This subject really gets me hot

1000 channels on TV but no on is addressing

The shameful reality

Oh my badd it's game time

We all rout for our favorite team
Baseball, basketball, football and hockey- oh

What's your favorite color?

Is it private care or public health?

I was recently faced with that decision

Although it was just another compromising position

Told me I need a biopsy, abnormal cells

Then in the same breath said we will see you in November

Wow, I look at my calendar it read June

And not to do the biopsy but to do another test

What's your favorite color?
Some wealth guy said he has all the answers

One thing for sure he knows how to create wealth

But what is his position about the poor?

The disenfranchised

The homeless

The low-test scores

Why are there not enough books to go around at some schools?

But then there are those with computers on every desk

Displacement seems common throughout every town

Judged by zip codes- where's the equality at?

Just clumps of disparity and disappoint remains

Suicide at an all-time high, families giving up

Smiles turned wrong side down

Too many people throwing in the towel

What's your favorite color?

Can we try wearing the same colors for a change?

Stop switching up colors

Let's try changing the rules of the game
Change, change, change

Spear change

Work for change

Live for change

Die for change

Time for change

This has been a public announcement

Change the channel

Atlanta's housewives coming through

Mindless amusement from a to z

Nene and Sheree showing out
Have you convinced their problems are true?

Did you forget they are in the 3%?

What's your favorite color?

Make sure you cast your vote
Many lives lost in the struggle to gain this right

So show up at the polls

And demand they do what's right!

Gloveless

This is what I do

I cause these words to serenade to you

Do I have your attention?

It may take some time

So don't try to find it in this rhyme

My place is not for a petite bath

I'm here to soak down deep, deep, deep into your mind

Like a sponge my desire is to soak up all your thoughts

Play with cupid's arrow until you get caught, behind

The sharp spear that whispers in your ear

From old school to new school, ballets and itunes

Keep up with the snap in new jack

Yea you desire a big pat on the back

Or should I sit in your lap

Dancing, I'll be your private dancer

No monies needed, I'll do it for fun

Sex in the City or in your ride

Pull up in the drive-in

Happy days are here to stay

Tickets to the show mystery, sci-fi or drama

Bring on comedy

Did I just wet my pants or is that a dream?

Expand on them, in detention

15 rounds in the ring, heavy weight champion

My heart is capable of more

And when you think of me

I want you to believe our paths were destine to cross

You fall to the floor, knock out.

Because the joy in my heart

It was once lost
The writings on the Wall

Was all that surgery necessary?
To get into My Space, Facebook, or on my channel

I'm trying to create something new, different and great

But just like playing chess, be careful of your next move

Return to Planet of the Apes

Perhaps a kiss, maybe a hug

But one thing for sure…
I'll be here to show you L O V E

Unconditional

You've cushioned me into what unconditional love is

What wrecked promises reek of?

What shattered dreams undergo

You've dispense me inconsistencies

I've tried to tell you respectfully

That the dream is vanishing

Promises don't appear satisfying

Is this what unconditional love is?

Must accept things?

Love you where you are?

Appreciate who you are?

Loving you unconditional

Or do I bid you far well

And love you from afar!

Who's watching?

The snow falls in the south

We are all astounded

The turbulence of waves coming by surprise

People scatter and nothing matters

There's no dodging disaster

And the skepticism of aftermath

Falling buildings, people buried….

Love ones left to morn

Claims made of mistrust, doubtful

That no one knew

Towns destroyed, bodies returned

Ashes to ashes, dust to dust

Is there anyone?

Is anyone paying attention?

As nature declares war

Perfect fit!

I'd pictured my success

I doubled my thoughts and made waves

Parted the red sea and ate the spoils

I give you permission to test me

But, I already pictured my success

Filled with countless delays and upsets

People will depart and seclusion approves

I predict that and worst

Doesn't matter it still won't halt me

You see I pictured my success

And if I tell you how it's going to be

You'll thrown a tantrum, push more problems my way

No need of informing you

Big baby in need of a napkin for your drool

Is that your best or is there more to you?

Just know that what you do

I allow

Keep up the good work

Must I remind you?

I've already pictured my success!

RAINBOW

Busy, flying from branch to branch
Gathering twigs and leaves,
Preparing a home indeed.

Pretty sounds fill the atmosphere,
Wings expand as it glides in mid-air.
Brilliant colors, blue, green and red,

And compliments of many shade in between

Plays peek-a-boo-difficult to spot as it hides, even when it sings sweet lullabies.

Who am I?
I am a Painted Bunting, no doubt.
A living rainbow, created to gladden your heart!

DARE TO BE MORE!

Aspire more

Believe more

Celebrate more

Desire more

Encourage more

Forgive more

Groove more

Help more

Inspire more

Jubilant more

Kiss more

Love more

Mediate more

Nourish more

Offer more

Perfect more

Quench more

Relax more

Surrender more

Trust more

Unite more

Write more

Xpect more

Yearn more

Zealous more

Always dare to be more!

Making A Fashion Statement

Write about it

1) Define what makes you unique?

2) How do you embrace your style?

3) List all the things you love about yourself?

*KEEP GOING AND DON'T GIVE UP!

RISKY BUSINESS

The Olympics are not designed for the weak.
Remember that as you triumphantly soar into your
Life's journey.
Go for the Gold in everything you do!
Believing the risk is worth the reward!

27 WAYS 2 LOVE

The number 27 is symbolic to 9 lives
Within the universe, I am run down by vultures and thieves
Trying to steal my heart and demolish my soul

Yet I flee

They try to seduce me with intoxicating pleasures
Offering me wicked and wore rags
That someone else has had
No thank you

I'll pass

Eyes glare, seducing stares
Consumed with an up rise but faced with a lock in
My heart is not for sell

I'll live for 27 ways 2 love

IN TIME

When I see you...

    Butterflies bring sunshine

    And bees make honey

    Lemonade drips down my back

When I see you

What Really Matters?

Being excited as soon as my feet hits the floor

Giving great praise to the Lord on bowed knees

Just excited- excited to be alive

It's the simple things

The humming of the birds

The winds breathe on my cheeks

The laughter of children playing

It's the simple things

A good morning text from my brother

A cup of tea with my Mother

A quick glance at family photos
It's the simple things

That makes life great, yet so often

Over looked

The sunrise and sunset

The clouds funny shape, so many

Flowers blooming, full of color

Friends catching up on lost time

And don't forget, yummy family dinners

It's the joy and love

In all of Gods beauty

Whether big or small

It's the simple things!

Promise

I promise to love you with all my heart
I give it to you freely
Ask for nothing in return

I promise to love you with all my soul
In that decision the truth came and I knew
God was in control

I promise to love you with every part of my being
You have stimulated, strengthen and applaud me
I can't image not giving you the very best of me

I promise to love you, honor and obey
I surrender the "I" in me in order for us to become one
In the site before God, our friends and family

I promise to love you mentally, spiritually, and physically
This is the merger that creates endless possibilities
This is the marriage that is meant to be!

What if?

What if I took a chance?
On sunshine, not leaving tan lines
Would the wave be worth the ride?

What if I took a chance?
On a flight oversees, defining gravity
Would be nice to end up in Belize?

What if I took a chance?
On my hopes and dreams, opposite of fear
Would the risk be worth the reward?

What if I took a chance?
On love, no more war
Would the joy be contagious, furious and grow?

What if …

LIVE AND LEARN

Young and dumb
Or
Older and hopeful

The stages of life are unique yet similar
We all travel our own path
Journey on into what we would like to believe is prosperity
Facing challenges in search for victory

But how do we rest?
Rest into the knowing that
Life is purposeful from the moment of conception
Beliefs, mostly passed down from generation to generation

Young and dumb
Or
Older and hopeful

Somehow, experiences don't always make it easy and less painful
As my mind closes the door to yet another relationship
I drift into tales of my own love chronicles

You know the kind that starts, hot and steamy, bodies melting like butter
Conversations seemingly have an insurmountable connection
Then somewhere between the kisses, backrubs and orgasms
Fallouts happens and everything get questioned

-Does he love me?

-Do I love him?

-Why did he do that?

-Why did I do this?

Hang-ups and break-ups

How do you spell relief?

How do you say another one bites the dust?

Love, just doesn't seem to last for me

But, through fall-out comes victory!

The victory of understanding myself just a little bit more

I'm learning my levels of tolerance, flexibility and endurance

My limits of saying enough is enough

And too much is way too much

I can make it without you

You can make it without me

Now what?

Picking myself

Dusting off myself

Young and dumb

Or

Older and hopeful

It is really all the same

We are trying to outlive the generational curse
Passed down and picked up unknowingly

So here's to those still listening
Let's journey into our own fantasies of—well
You decide, remembering that the curse has been broken
We no longer have to live in the shadows of what our parents did
Let's live, live, and live
Believing that there is so much to give
And love, love, and love

Through all that's said and done
Whether young and dumb

Or older and hopeful
Stick around because surely the best is yet to come!

Pure

You have loved me pass my indiscretions and faults

You have watched over me without a second thought

You have cared for me without hesitation

You have provide for me seeking no compensation

You have protected me through victory and defeat

Your love can't ever be beat

Thank you God

My Father and friend

Your love leaves indications of how it never ends!

TESTING TESTING

To have a broken heart

To have shattered dreams

To have misplaced my notes of remembering how to breathe

When all seems to unravel and crumble apart

I still search for my notes

So I can recall how to play this part

To be sad from within

My back begins to ache

I just want to stop looking for my notes

And give into the painful heartbreak

But the giant inside of me

Refuses to play along

She insist that I keep on looking

Reminding me that I must find a way

To sing my song

To be sad, lonely and depressed

Is the reason why I must find my notes

So I can breath

Long after this test!

YOU SMELL THAT?

Catching dreams with nightmares
Good times with bad times as missiles deploy
And cosmic skies open up drip, drip
Dripping down pixy dust

Allured into the manure of fake smells
Kisses that whisper shhhh don't tell
And boys wearing stilettos as they sache'
Across ballroom floors

Did you see that coming?

All this free lib and secret chatter
From the white house to the penthouse
From the pentagon to the synagogue

Penises have become pussies
You smell that … manure up to your waist
Put your boots on so you don't get step on
Into the shit with your skirt on
Polka dots rub off and white spots disappears

Did you hear that?
Balls drop- tits tide down
Baggy pants, hand sways back and forth
Did you see that coming- Belinda has become Clay?

Now what the hell for?

You smell that… manure up to your waist

Mixed up genders want to surrender, to
Outcries and mad eyes of knock off love affairs
Winds whispers sour smells of confusion

Confusion, confusion confusing

You smell that.. Manure up to your waist
Mommy's become daddy's and
Daddy's become mommies in private spaces

Our children they can't distinguish who is who
Our children can't make out who is who
Our children, we are confusing our Children

The manures getting thick
Bone, chicken bone, red bone,

A bag of weed no I said weave
It's all coming undone
It's insanity not make-believe
Tighten up or take it out!

From the pulpit to parking lot
From Sunday schools to sandboxes

The manure is thick
And like quick sand

If you're not careful that's when you'll sink in.
Is that the Devil's plan?

Blinders off so you don't get caught in
Charlotte's Web
I hear that's the name they call you on the streets
You hand out happy endings being reckless
Knowing your name is really Chester.

Chester- married with 3 kids and a baby on the way
My, my, my just what would your Momma say

Manure up to your waist
You smell that???

.COM

When I decided it was you, there was nothing left to say

When I convinced myself that your touch was the best touch

It was out of my hands that very same day

When I smiled from the inside out, it left no questionable doubt

It was you.com

You are the one!

Not just any one but the one

The one that makes me giggle, brings on that certain wiggle

I don't have to pretend when that certain feeling hits me

Because you know just where to pinch me

Yea you are the one.com

You are my feel good goody powder, taking away all the aches and pains

You are my best cup of coffee down to the last drop... the energy I need to run all day

You are the best book to read, a definite page-turner, number 1 bestseller

Words running off the page

Yea you are the one.com

You are my favorite meal complete with all the trimmings and dessert on the side

You are the best back rub after a long ride

You are my cooler in hot places either in the boardroom or on the field playing

You are the conductor, instructor, always operating in one accord

You are that one and only

That man of my life
The one, I've truly been waiting for

You are that one.com

And I don't think you even know it
Because you are so low key, smooth and don't show it

It's no question the way you are dipped in high caliber

Wheels turning on all cylinders-click

That one thing that makes you it

Yea your stature is stupendous and your mystique is mysterious

Your smile is stunning and your style is simple

But the secret is under all those layers

Like a baker stacks cake and a banker stacks cheese

You are the one.com

Like the lawn-man rakes leaves

Yea, you are the one who turns my soul over day after day

You are the one.com

Better than the best soap opera, short story, Oscar winner or show stopper

You are no match for Jerry Springer, Oprah or rest his soul, Frank Sinatra

They can't compare with you and all the things you do for me

You are the one.com

Turn off the radio, TV, and bright lights in the big city

The way you shine Edison would be jealous

Because you are that one to me.com

Risky Business

Write about it

1) Create your bucket list:

2) What makes you happy?

3) Who are the people you enjoy being with and why?

*KEEP GOING AND DON'T GIVE UP!

Who Moved My Dream???

Hey have you seen it??
My zeal, my zest my reason to breathe?
Just as soon as life gets easy- the complications,
Soon begins!

AWAKENING

Behind steel bars, doors slam

Piercing reverberations impair my ears

Barking and whistling, hands beckon

I view it as a compliment, a welcoming jester

So I nod my head, and then turn away

Awaken, deficient of sunlight

Just that steel door slamming back

Rigid arctic faces, no smiles attached

Shouts of get up!

Mixed with disrespectful insults.

Somewhere between following commands, my mind expands
Awakened to the opportunity, I began

They can fracture me physically and rough me up mentally

But spiritually, their steps depart taking its shadow

So as the light becomes absent, and the sound softens

My thoughts will align with desires of my heart

By letting the Lord employ me, even in a place so dark.

DAY DREAMS

Peek a boo's in

And night sleeps on

When you picture more than what you see

Raindrops down

And rainbows up

Do you see, golden vessel at the end?

Stirring in the pot

Putting in what you seeking, out

No rules, no restrictions, no boundaries

That's the lovely thing about a dream!

Me

I splash on the surveys

Please hold the applause

Bold and bright colors

Changing circumstances for once and for all

One stroke, two stroke, three…

Signing my name

What is it called?

Simply, called me!

HIGHER LEARNING

Seeds of solitude saturate my urge

So I'll seek to ascertain my fate

Traveling halls, roll calls

My hand is raised

Questions needing answers

Please call on me!

ALL ABOARD

Enter into the maze of life's own findings

Hide and seek

Hunted and captured are the discoveries of ones own journey

To imagine ones destiny can bring satisfaction to the thought

Unlimited pleasure and countless creations

Satisfying mood swings

unleashing ravishing revelations

All aboard…

Are you all in?

Will you commit to your passion?

Or surrender to you circumstances?

Admission is certain, cash in your ticket

Pack up your thoughts

Last call,

All aboard?

FALLEN

Is it surrendering?

Or is it captivity?

Our love is meant to be!

MISTAKEN IDENTITY

Mistaken Identity
Too tired to run
I've been spotted all over town
But I haven't left the room

She looks like me
She sounds like me, too
But my shadow stays put
Not going anywhere

Many years ago someone stopped by
Made off with my joy
And left me busted inside

He promised he would always make me smile
Only touch me gently
And kisses so sweet and lots of love inside
But that was just a lie

Though he stayed in my bed
He murdered my delight
It's been a long time, since things felt right

So there is no way I've be spotted
Laughing and dancing last night
Because, I don't know how to leave!

Years have left lines

And marked up my sprit

Tears crystallized

Would be nice if I knew how to leave

I would find happy thoughts and bundle them up

And put on my dancing shoes, too

Avoid countless trips to the hospitals

Of being bandaged and abused

If only I know how to leave!

COMMITTED

He asked her, "What do you want?"

Her reply, "I want it all"

He responded, puzzled look on his face

"What does that mean?"

Her answers aren't clear

He misreads her

But, he loves her

So he'll keep asking

LIVING

Words of wisdom, breeding actions of success

Building monuments of historical bridges

Tested, tried and true

While surrendering to roads less traveled

Embarking on adventures

Learning from each experience

Its life

So, live it!

I AM ENOUGH

I heard it said that we work on our dreams so we can thrive,

If not we will work on someone else's then we will die.

Let me introduce myself to you,

I am Wanda D Hollis

The D is for Denise the name given to me by my grandmother and Wanda was a name my Great Grandmother wanted to me to have. My family call me WD and others refer to me as Wanda D,

So there you have I AM Wanda D Hollis.

Either way I am just passing through

I came by to inspire you

To live beyond your dreams

Go pass the clouds and travel on Mars

If that's what you so desire to do

Let me assure you

I truly believe in you

Your visions and hopes and seeds planted in you

Put there for a reason, perfectly designed for you

I believe that the universe is simply waiting on you

You see I didn't always know that truth
Then one day I woke up
And I saw my greatness staring back at me

It gave me the courage to believe and see
What others had seen in me
What others had encouraged me to be

You see I didn't always feel I was good enough
So I dabbled and played around with my talent and dreams
Didn't think I could make the cut
Then I discovered, I am enough

I am enough!

And not because I live life perfectly
I often break the rules
But then I finally decided
To take greater chances
Determined to take the shackles off
My voice, my hands, and my heart

Celebrating freedom

Knowing and believing that I am enough
I am free to be all
Yes... all that god has planned and planted for me

Like a bird that soars with no instructions, it just comes naturally

For my gift is to inspire through these words

I hope you comprehend that my only mission it to encourage you

Let me ask you 4 questions…

1. What are your desires?
2. What is that thing, you know that think that burns inside of you?
3. That thing that nags you?
4. What is that dream that use to ride you?

I am here to tell you

I am here to encourage you

I am here to let you know that it is not to late

To take your dream off the shelve and give birth

Let it kiss the earth

And then spread it as though it was a dessert

I am enough

I am enough

You are enough

We win together

Woven in the tapestry of love

It is the thread and we are the bread that feeds the masses

It is our gifts that changes classes

Don't take the semester off

School is still in session

With the strength of Malcolm X, Dr. King, and Harriett Tubman, Langston

Hughes, and My ancestors
Pride, strength, tenacity
And with the capacity running through my veins
For the magnitude of MY vision does not compete with fame

It encompasses all that I am
No price tags, or expiration dates
It is the energy from the universe that impregnates
To leave my imprint on you in a very unique way

You see, I am enough
You are enough
If you choose to believe

I recall when I was a little girl
My momma told me I was Beautiful, Smart, and I could do
Anything, I wanted to

Those words have played over and over in my mine and in my heart
It just took me a little while to understand the totality of the sound
Yes I will say that again
It just took me a little while to understand the totality of the sound

So, here I stand ready and willing to take my mountain

And move to new ground
And though the soil may be hard and work involved
I would only disappoint you, if

I didn't show up to bless you

It is only my duty to prove to you
That the greatest person you see
Your reflection, and it always stares back at you

I am enough
I am enough
You are enough

Yes, you are enough

Now live

Knowing and believing that there is nothing

Absolutely nothing…you can't do!
Why… because we are enough
And together we are more than enough!

Who Moved My Dream???

Write about it

1) Are you living your dream??? If not why?

2) Think back when you were a child what did you want to be and why?

3) What fears are holding you back from pursing your dream?

*KEEP GOING AND DON'T GIVE UP!

107 DAILY AFFIRMATIONS TO LIVE BY

I am only listening to the Joy Bells ringing in my mind.

They have my full permission to play over and over again!

107 DAILY AFFIRMATIONS TO LIVE BY

1.   I am free to be a creative as I choose to be

2.   I am reliable, smart and full of energy

3.   I am in charge of my happiness

4.   I owe myself the best life possible

5.   I keep a SMILE on my face

6.   I always make time to celebrate the small things

7.   I expect good health

8.   I am rich in all things good

9.   I am living life passionately

10.   I am learning all that is necessary for me to grow

11.   I am fulfilling GODS vision and plan for my life

12.   I am in a joyous state of mind

13.   I am always good to my body

14.   I am attracting the best relationships to my life

15.   I always spread LOVE

16.   I am expecting an exceptional day today

17.   I am expecting all the favor to exceed my expectations

18.   I am always building quality relationships

19.   I am eating foods that provide me optimum health

20.   I am CELEBRATING every moment of the day

21.   I am doing what I love

22.   I am sharing my talents with the world

23.   I speak words that will create my dreams

24.   I take action on my written plan

25.   I am experiencing POSTIVE results

26.   My day is good and getting better

27.   I am a blessing to others

28.   I am accepting those who want to bless my life

29.   I am the perfect giver of love, kindness and gratitude

30.   I BELIEVE in my dream
31.   I make plans and work my plans daily

32.   I am a winner

33.   I help others become winners

34.   I am my best cheerleader

35.   I FOCUS on why not how to get the job done

36.   I do what is necessary to succeed in my business

37.   I know the pain will pass

38.   I quit doing my best now I do what is necessary

39.   I picture my DREAM coming true each moment of the day

40.   I am all love from head to toe

41.   What I am looking for is looking for me
42.   Love is over taking me

43.   It is DONE

44. I save myself first

45. I am a champion

46. I am feeling beautiful

47. I am strong

48. I am on my way up

49. My SUCESS is a decision

50. Believe, Believe, Believe

51. I will not be denied

52. No excuses only solutions

53. I have all the monies I need to live the life I DESIRE
54. I have to participate in my own rescue

55. All I need is within me now

56. All the JOY is within me now

57. What I focus on will expand

58. Thoughts, feeling, and actions are what changes situations

59. I APPRECIATE all of my experiences

60. I understand my greatness

61. On one can beat me loving myself

62. Being grateful is most important

63. I am surrounded with love and beauty

64. Love PRODUCES love

65. I am big love
66. I give big love

67. I never give up on my dream

68. I am blessed, healthy, wealthy and wise

69. PRODUCTION not promises brings on changes

70. I am inspired by my failures

71. I make sure I'm always studying what I want to become

72. I am filled with passion and purpose

73. WINNERS make a way- winners make noise

74. My thoughts drive my behavior

75. I raise my actions and raise my results

76. I am grateful for my family
77. I am grateful for my job

78. I am Thankful for my children

79. I am grateful for my childhood

80. My greatest gift is LOVE

81. My greatest power is forgiveness

82. I don't set out to prove others wrong only to prove myself better

83. TEAMWORK makes the dream work

84. I stay open minded to opportunities

85. I am trusting my inner senses

86. I am beautiful

87. I am enough

88. I am DESIGNING my life
89. I accept my defeats knowing I will just start over again

90. I will keep trying until I get it right

91. I will never quit believing in myself

92. I am motivating myself

93. I am willing to take chances

94. I am UNSTOPPABLE

95. I always say kind things to people

96. I am always inspiring others

97. I am Gods Child and no weapon formed against me will harm me

98. I am expecting a miracle today

99. I am expecting a financial BLESSING today

100. I am expecting a favorable medical report today

101. I am expecting to receive favor in business today

102. I am expecting my mind to flow with great ideas today

103. I am provided with resources to solve any setback

104. I am a MIRACLE

105. I am trusting in God

106.   I forgive myself

107.   I am not judging others, I only accept with LOVE

Affirm Your Decisions

We all make choices, even when we choose not to make a decision we are indeed making one. I celebrate with you in YOUR decision to decide to live a life of happiness, bravery and adventure!

You are ENOUGH to fulfill your divine purpose!

I want to leave you with a few tips:

1) Affirm your lifestyle daily

2) Surround yourself with people that support your dream

3) Do something fun that requires you to laugh

4) Forgive yourself and others quickly

5) Take responsibility for yourself

6) Love and respect yourself

7) Always be thankful for another day

About the Author

As native of Detroit Michigan, Wanda D. Hollis has been blazing the trail as an entrepreneur for two decades. She has been involved in countless business ventures from health and wellness to real estate, from traditional businesses to network marketing business alike. She is a natural at inspiring others to follow their hearts and dreams, also she never short of offering encouraging words.

Hollis first started writing as a journalist in Pershing High School. This is where she first discovered her ability to capture readers through words. It was in those early days that she originally thought of becoming a journalist. Which in fact did guide her to enroll in college to study communication at Oakland University, but dropped out after her first year to start her very first business in network marketing. It was during these years that she developed the proficiency of building relationships and speaking in public. She is known throughout the business community as being a quality resource of connecting people together. A true outside the box thinker, always thinking of innovative was together people together.

She is the founder and host of Wanda D-TV, a platform designed to bridge the community together. Her guest have included people of varies backgrounds from politicians to painters allowing them to voice whatever is going on in their world. In February of 2011 Hollis was the emcee for the American Poet-GA Sport, a poetry contest produces by Alice Shapiro, Poet Laureate of Douglasville Ga. She has spoke at several organization including The Caribbean and American Business Connections, Partners in Education, When Beauty Calls, Detroit Urban League, Mothers Against Drunk Driving and Empowering Change Network, just to name a few. Whether she is speaking to children or adults she is guaranteed to deliver with excitement and enthusiasm. Her antics will hold your attention and the message is always heartfelt.

In 2014 Hollis founded Walking Through The Storm LLC, Atlanta's premiere lifestyle development and coaching company for businesses and individuals. Offering a full portfolio of networking events and seminars, workshops and classes, mentoring and accountability. WTTS also offer sales and customer service training including business support services.

Hollis is available as a keynote speaker, emcee, an organizer for workshops and seminars. She is also an experienced trainer in sales, customer service and marketing optimization. To contact Hollis directly at wordsrpower@gmail.com and visit www.wttsempowers.com.

www.ingramcontent.com/pod-product-compliance
Lightning Source LLC
LaVergne TN
LVHW021516080426
835509LV00018B/2537